Dedicated to my children

ISBN 978-1-7363010-0-5
Published By Highway550 Books

highway550.com

Miles of Age

By
Stephen Smith

Highway550 Books

The *Solitary Birthday ride* is a common bicycling activity and a challenge of my local bicycle shop. The goal of the day is to ride your age in miles, by yourself, on your birthday... a chance to reflect on the past and plan for the future.

For me, with a June Birthday, the challenge is the heat and the storms... oh, and the number of miles.

This challenge was on the Katy Trail...a good way to start the next decade.

The weather would be a factor and I was soon to find out the road surface would be a factor as well. The starting point was the Boonville, Missouri Trailhead of the Katy Trail. The route was to ride west in an *out and back*.
I had tools and mechanical supplies packed in the panniers.

I was prepared.
I was ready.

Boonville to Pilot Grove

I was at the Boonville trail head.

It had stormed most of the night.

   It was a bit damp...
     It wasn't hot... yet
       and the trail surface looked wet.

I put on my helmet, raingear, and gloves
then I looked over my checklist.

The odometer was reading zero !

Water bottles full ✓

Snacks ✓

Raingear ✓

Tools ✓

Spare tubes ✓

Camera ✓

Sun Screen ✓

Tire Pressure ✓

I was ready.

I started the ride.

This is a great trail but the dampness of the trail was apparent, and my tires seemed to sink in the trail gravel. It was hard to go fast.

But that was fine, I had to be careful not to go too fast ... I did not want to fall. The odometer was showing my speed about 11 mph.

The trail tree canopy was amazing!

I was off and feeling good as a few miles fell behind me. As my pace settled, I started recalling the early years of my life...and smiling...

   ...With each mile, I recalled each year.

This was going to be a great birthday ride!

Then ... I encountered a huge obstacle.

   Just like life,
         there are always obstacles to overcome.

The big overnight storm had blown down giant tree branches that now covered the trail. I was able to walk my bicycle around the branches. There was no way that I could have moved the branches off the trail. That would have taken a chainsaw.

I was able to continue riding but worried about what other obstacles I may encounter.

Off in the distance, I heard vehicle noise.

As I rode, the noise got louder and I discovered I was about to go over an Interstate Highway. I rode high above it on the Katy Trail railroad bridge and stopped to take a picture.

I thought it was a perfect metaphor of how some people go much faster than others.

I was thankful that today I was riding a bicycle and not in a hurry driving on the Interstate Highway.

As with life, there is always 'another obstacle' to overcome, though some are easier to overcome than others.

I encountered a number of fallen trees and branches. You always need to take care overcoming the obstacles so you do not create more issues.

After the recent storm, there were a lot of branches down. The smaller branches needed to be avoided when riding as they had a tendency to get in the spokes or flip up and cut my legs.

There was a very large branch that covered the trail about ten miles into the ride. I had to lift my bicycle over it because it was too large for me to move. The trail maintenance crew would be busy removing the debris after the overnight storm.

First Stop, Pilot Grove.

As with life, the first 12 years/miles went by fast...

... and were fun.

Even though the ride, so far, was a bit of an uphill climb, I hardly noticed.

Oh, if only life would be that easy and fun.

The scenery was so beautiful on this first stretch. And, the birds were everywhere singing great songs.

I added some water to my bottles then continued on my way. So far, so good.

From Pilot Grove, I continued west on the Katy Trail.

I thought about my years and miles as I rolled on. At this point, I was in my 'teen years'.

Those years were a bit more challenging and the ride was a bit more difficult too.

A few more water breaks,
A few more snack breaks,
A few more stops for resting and pictures.

The birds continued to sing and little animals scurried across the trail. It was all very enjoyable.

Yes, when you are riding, you never know what you might find.

With the early miles on the Katy Trail came ups and downs, just like life itself...

    ... full of 'ups and downs',

        but oh the views ...

and the places and experiences along the way!

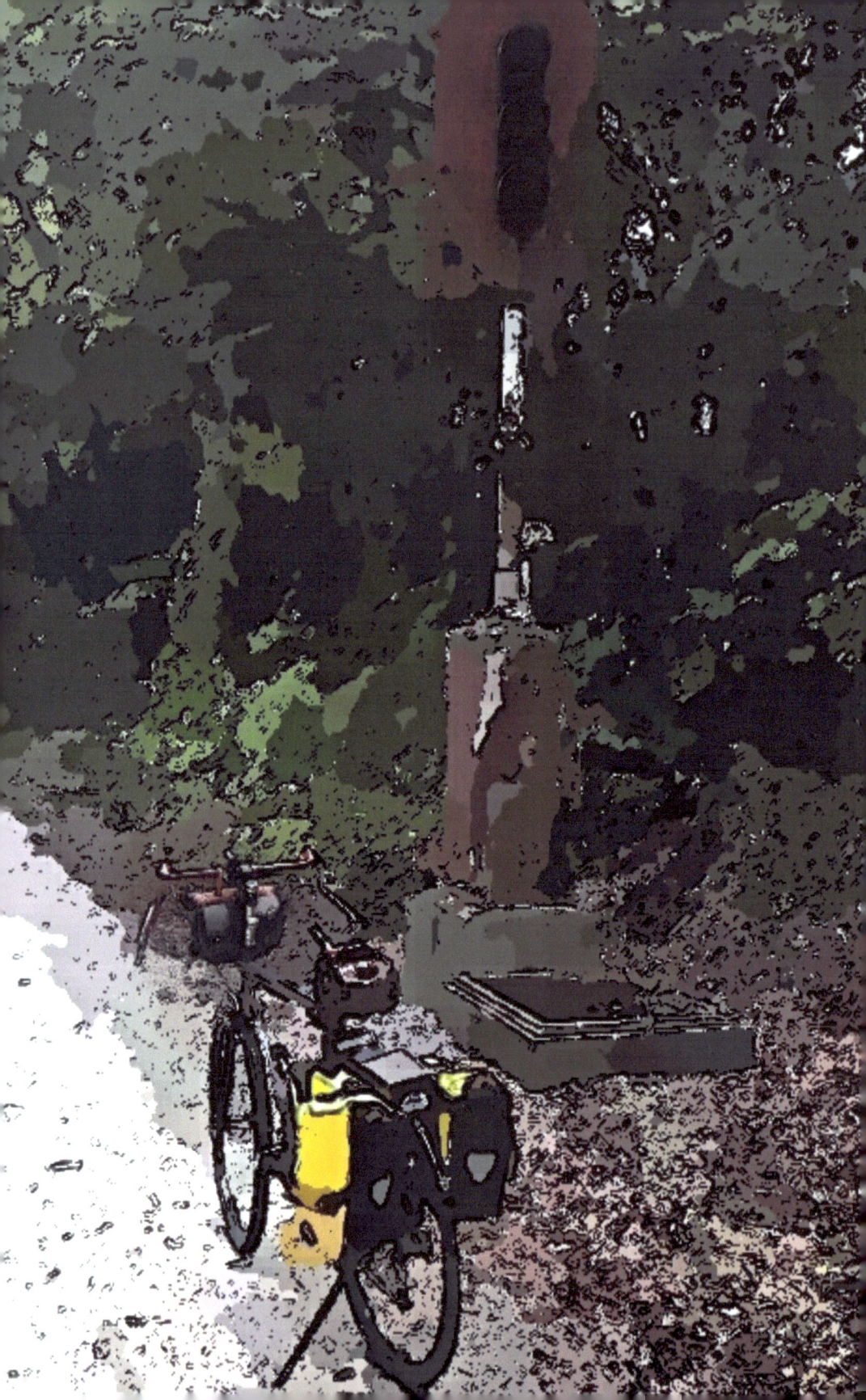

Riding on the Katy Trail is filled with wonders to be discovered. All bicycle routes give the opportunity to see unique things, but seeing an old railroad signal at the side of the trail is one of my favorite sights.

As I looked at the old railroad signal, I imagined the years of service it gave when the Katy Railroad was active. This old railroad signal is a truly appreciated artifact that survived the *Rails to Trails* conversion.

A picture stop for sure.
… and time for a little water break and a snack.

.

The Katy Trail surface started to dry as the day got warmer. No longer needing the light jacket, I made a stop at mile marker 216 for some clothing adjustments.

It is the special signs you notice along the way that have meaning and the mile markers call out the miles as you pedal by. You always remember the special times and events of your life on birthday rides. Each year the ride gets one mile longer and one year more special.

As I left mile marker 216, I realized the halfway point of the ride would be coming soon.

After the mile marker 216 water break, and now having a drier trail surface, I started to pick up the pace.

Soon I looked down at the odometer and saw ...

30 miles! ...

Halfway there !

Shaver Creek

30 miles in.

Now it was major decision time.

This journey was an *out and back,* so I needed to decide
when to turnaround.

I felt good, but I was hungry.

If I kept going, in six miles (about a 1/2 hour) I would
arrive at a town where I could eat, rest, then start the
journey back. But that would put me at plus seventy miles
for the day and add at least one more hour to the trip.

If I turned around at thirty miles, it would be about two
hours to get back to Pilot Grove. But that would mean I
would not be eating for two hours.

The decision process is always interesting.
You always hope you will make the right one ...

    ...because after that, it's just water under the bridge.

I decided to continue on so I could eat sooner.

After riding one and one half miles, I stopped at mile
marker 222 and did a quick calculation. I realized that I
would be short on time unless I turned around immediately.

So I turned around and headed back.

Eight miles later and now really hungry, I started the forties
on the odometer.
.

In the 40's, riding started to get hard.
Each mile felt like it was uphill, and going uphill was slow.

I was going slow. I needed to make frequent stops and it
was depressing. My body seemed to hurt with every push
of the pedal. Downhill gives a feeling of euphoria but there
were few downhill moments in this part of the Katy Trail.
Being hungry and hurting made it a slow struggle.

I kept thinking and hoping Pilot Grove would appear
around the next corner, but no ...
        ... so I kept riding, and riding.

Eventually Pilot Grove was around the next corner. That is
where I found the boost I needed. It was a cheeseburger at
a local restauraunt!

The food and a short rest were perfect.
Pilot Grove is a great place with nice people.

Ready to continue, I looked at my odometer. It showed
that I was in the early fifties.

Now feeling refreshed, riding to my sixty mile goal was enjoyable. It is amazing what a bit of a rest and a cheeseburger will do for your energy and ease of riding. It was exciting approaching the sixty mile mark on my odometer.

I saw a turtle crossing the road. I usually stop to take a picture of a turtle and then move it off the trail for their safety. Instead, I told him to just carry on as I rode by. As with life, sometimes it is best to not interfere.
Anyway, I was on a mission!

I rode past a wounded bird walking down the trail that was struggling to get out of the way. As I rode past, I wished it luck. There was not much else that I could have done, anyway.

At fifty eight miles, a stick went into the front wheel spokes, then came out with a snap. I noticed that the speedometer/odometer had stopped.

"NO .. Not NOW"   I yelled out to nobody .....

 I stopped and was able to adjust the magnet attachment.
The odometer started working again.
Oh, the little things that make you panic.

A few minutes later the odometer rolled to **60** miles.
        I paused for the photo.
        I felt good.
        I felt good about the ride and myself.

But the ride was not yet over...
        ... not until I got back to the Boonville Trail Head.

The next three miles went by in the blink of an eye.

    ... *such is life*.

I arrived back at the Boonville Trail Head from which I started.

The odometer read 63 miles.

It was a strange hot day... about eighty degrees, but with 75% humidity, it was *strange*. I brought 4 water bottles and some snacks, but really should have brought more food.

Overall, it was a great ride on my Surly Long Haul Trucker. I averaged about 11 miles an hour... not fast, but enjoyable, and on the wet road surface, that speed was not too bad for me. The Surly LHT is not fast, but is a very comfortable old friend. I have traveled over 20,000 miles since buying it long ago.

    If you get a chance, I recommend a solitary

    Age of Miles
    Birthday ride.

    Enjoy every minute, enjoy every mile